L & L Hawaiian Barbecue Cookbook

By

Eddie Flores, Jr.

Illustrated By
Jon J. Murakami

®

ISBN 978-0-9858192-0-0

Book Design: Brandon Dela Cruz
Illustrations: Jon J. Murakami

Published by:
L & L Franchise, Inc.
931 University Avenue, Suite 202
Honolulu, Hawaii 96826
Phone: 808-951-9888
Fax: 808-951-0888
Email: info@hawaiianbarbecue.com
Website: www.hawaiianbarbecue.com
Facebook: www.facebook.com/hawaiianbarbecue
Twitter: www.twitter.com/hawaiianbbq
YouTube: http://www.youtube.com/hawaiianbarbecue

Dedication

To my lovely wife, Elaine, a vegetarian who refuses to eat at L & L Hawaiian Barbecue, and my two daughters, Elisia and Ellice, who crave for the onolicious Hawaiian Barbecue over their mother's bland vegan cooking.

"The Family Man"

Da Boss Collecting His Cut

"The lucky L & L customer at PICO RIVERA in CALIFORNIA won $266 million dollars. Maybe he give away free laulau, poke, and lomi salmon." Danny, Pico Rivera

Why Named $266 Million Winning Lottery Recipes?

In May 6, 2010, Gilbert Cisneros bought a lottery ticket at the L & L Hawaiian Barbecue in Pico Rivera, California and won $266 million dollars in one of the largest mega million lottery jackpots in history. Gilbert was in downtown to pick up his wife, Jackie Cisneros. She had a craving for a KFC double-decker chicken. Instead, Gilbert stopped by his favorite L & L Hawaiian Barbecue for BBQ chicken and also bought a lottery ticket. Six hours later, the Cisneros won the $266 Million Mega lottery.

The food at L & L Hawaiian Barbecue must be a godsend. (No offense to KFC). The L & L menu is a collection of Hawaii's tastiest dishes. Combined with Jon J. Murakami's funny illustrations, I know you will find this cookbook very entertaining. Not only will you get the secret Hawaiian Barbecue recipes, you will laugh heartily while you are eating. Who knows.... you might be the next $266,000,000 Mega Million lottery winner when you cook with L & L Hawaiian Barbecue winning lottery recipes!

L & L Office at Work

Acknowledgements

Thanks to my office staff for their support: Ellice Flores, Caroline Guira, Kelly Gan, Andrew Lee, Kanoe Fragas, Scotty Cheong, Johnson Kam, Christina Kam, Raymond Cheng, Josie Akana, Brandon Dela Cruz, Bryan Andaya and Elaine Flores.

Thanks to Chef Raymond Cheng for his secret recipes, Brandon Dela Cruz for his design, Ellice Flores for the fan mails, and Josie Akana, Bryan Andaya and Elisia Flores for their editing.

Thanks to Jon J. Murakami for his funny illustrations. Jon created most of L & L's Hawaiian t-shirts and the yearly Chinese zodiac calendars. He is an artist who can capture Hawaii's people and scenes with humor and sensitivity.

Thanks to Gilbert and Jackie Cisneros for winning the $266,000,000 Mega Millions Jackpot and buying the winning ticket at L & L Hawaiian Barbecue, Pico Rivera, California.

Special thanks reserved for my wife, Elaine, and my two daughters, Elisia and Ellice, for their patience, love, understanding, and encouragement during this arduous endeavor.

Contributors

Brandon T. Dela Cruz is Director of Marketing for L & L. With talent on loan from God, he has grown a considerable amount of white hair since working for Eddie. He was given the title "Hawaii's Most Eligible Filipino Bachelor" by Hawaii's Filipino community. (Un)fortunately, he still holds the title to this day.

Josie Akana is Director of Franchising for L&L. Under Eddie's wing, she has acquired great skills and experience in entrepreneurship, sales and marketing. A woman of faith, Josie is a living miracle – thanks to the lives of six chickens – a long story!

Bryan Andaya is Vice President and Chief Operating Officer of L & L Franchise, Inc. An attorney by training, Bryan can hardly believe his job is to spread two scoops of Aloha (i.e., the plate lunch) to the world. Bryan and his wife, Mary Ann, hope this passion for the islands will inspire their children, Avalyne and Alyna, to pursue great things in life while appreciating the unique aspects of Hawaii.

Raymond Cheng is Executive Chef of L & L. Known as the "Grand Daddy" of the L & L franchisees, Raymond is instrumental in the operation and expansion of L & L's worldwide.

Table of Contents

Table of Contents (continued)

The Beginning of L & L

L & L started as L & L Dairy which was named after the owner, Robert Lee Sr. and his son, Robert Lee, Jr. It was the third largest dairy on Oahu in the 1950's. L & L Dairy sold milk, juice, eggs, bread, ice cream, and butter. The dairy's output had slightly higher butterfat content, and tasted richer than other dairy products.

In 1959, Mr. Lee sold L & L Dairy to the Hirayama brothers. They converted L & L into a dairy fountain and changed the name to L & L Dairy Liliha Fountain. In the 1960's, L & L changed hands and names several times. Eventually, Mrs. Kitagawa sold L & L to Eddie Flores in 1976 as L & L Drive-Inn.

Eddie Flores lived two blocks away from L & L Drive-Inn on Liliha Street. As a student at the University of Hawaii, Eddie loved to stop by L & L to enjoy a beef curry plate lunch. When Eddie graduated in 1970, he started Sun Pacific Realty, a real estate company that specialized in listing and selling businesses. In 1976, Eddie listed L & L Drive-Inn for sale for $22,000. Two months later, he decided to buy the restaurant and gave it as a gift to his parents, Eduardo and Margaret Flores. Eddie asked his friend, Johnson Kam, to partner with him so his mother did not have to work in the evenings. A few years later, Margaret decided to retire from the restaurant business. Eddie sold his interest to Johnson. Under Johnson's ownership, he expanded the menu and added many items such as BBQ chicken and chicken katsu. Thereafter, Johnson opened two other locations, on University Avenue and in Chinatown.

Johnson is known for his generosity. He helped and permitted several of his friends to use the name L & L Drive-Inn without charging a fee or royalty. In 1988, Johnson and Eddie's families were vacationing in Maui. Eddie told Johnson that he could expand the L & L brand by forming a franchise and charging a royalty. Johnson agreed and they started a new partnership to expand and franchise L & L Drive-Inn.

Expanding to Continental U.S.

In March of 1991, Eddie and Johnson formed L & L Franchise, Inc. and started to officially franchise in Hawaii. Eddie was named the President and CEO, while Johnson was the Chairman. The L & L chain grew from 5 locations to more than 40 restaurants in less than 10 years. In November 1999, L & L expanded to the Mainland as L & L Hawaiian Barbecue. Derryck and Elaine Tom moved from Honolulu to open the first franchise in the City of Industry, California. Other locations followed and with each one came a throng of Hawaiian expatriates willing to wait in long lines just to taste L & L Hawaiian Barbecue. For instance, it was snowing on the day L & L opened in Dallas, Texas. There was no press release or advertisement. By word of mouth alone, 100 people were waiting in line when the Dallas L & L opened its doors. Today, there are close to 200 locations stretching from Honolulu to New York City, as well as Japan, New Zealand, China, and American Samoa. You need only read the fan mail in this book to understand L&L's phenomenal success and why L & L Hawaiian Barbecue is the #1 restaurant in Hawaii.

What is Hawaiian Barbecue?

L & L Drive-Inn's menu includes the famous Hawaiian favorite known as "plate lunch." The meal includes two scoops of rice, one scoop of macaroni salad, and a main entrée such as chicken, beef, or pork. The history of plate lunch dates back to the plantation days before World War II. Various ethnic groups such as the Chinese, Filipinos, Japanese, Portuguese and Hawaiians worked together and shared their food. The meals included teriyaki beef, teriyaki chicken, sweet and sour pork, adobo, noodles, etc.

Hawaiian Barbecue was not previously known as a Hawaiian dish. When Eddie expanded L & L Drive-Inn to the Mainland in 1991, he decided that "plate lunch" was too foreign a term for Mainland consumers. So instead, Eddie renamed the dish and the restaurant, L & L Hawaiian Barbecue, and this is how, with a few exceptions, the brand is known and loved today.

To find the L & L Hawaiian Barbecue locations closest to you, please check out the L & L website at www.hawaiianbarbecue.com or email info@hawaiianbarbecue.com.

Ask for KATSU and Not CAT-SU

"ENOUGH!!! I miss you guyz from FARGO, ND. Freezing and lonely. I need your L & L Grindz, laulau, kalua pork and whatever you have." Dave, Wausau

Chicken Katsu

Serves 5 to 6 people

Ingredients

- 1 egg
- 1 cup of cornstarch
- 1/2 cup of water
- 1 teaspoon of salt
- 1/2 teaspoon of white pepper
- 1/2 teaspoon of garlic powder
- 1/2 teaspoon of sesame oil
- 2 pounds of skinless chicken (butterfly)
- 2 cups of panko*

Steps

1. Combine and mix ingredients except chicken and panko in a bowl to make a paste.
2. Marinate chicken for 10 minutes with the paste.
3. Coat with panko.
4. Deep fry for 2 to 3 minutes or until golden brown.

*For best tasting deep fried chicken katsu, use Upper Crust panko.

Vegans are Hot

"Reason #1 why I can't be a vegetarian: chicken katsu and laulau."
Richard, San Jose

Hawaiian Barbecue Chicken

Serves 5 to 6 people

Ingredients

- 2 to 2-1/2 pounds of boneless chicken thighs (butterfly)
- 1 quart of teriyaki sauce*
- 1 tablespoon of soy sauce
- Dash of sesame seed oil

Steps

1. Combine and mix all ingredients in a pot for 2 hours.
2. Heat pan to medium heat with sesame seed oil.
3. Put chicken thighs skin side first for 2 to 3 minutes.
4. Flip chicken thigh and cook for another 2 to 3 minutes or until it is done.

*See page 105 for the teriyaki sauce recipe

Dumb Sheep

"Thank you so much for branching to New Zealand, it brings so much memories of my first trip to Honolulu five years ago." J.T. and Shari, Auckland

Lemon Chicken

Serves 5 to 6 people

Ingredients

- 1/4 cup of flour
- 1 cup of corn starch
- 1/2 cup of water
- 1 teaspoon of salt
- 1 teaspoon of white pepper
- 2 eggs
- 1 tablespoon of sesame seed oil
- 2 to 2-1/2 pounds of boneless chicken thighs (butterfly)
- Vegetable oil

Steps

1. Combine and mix flour, corn starch, water, salt, pepper, eggs and sesame seed oil in a bowl to make a paste.
2. Marinate chicken in a bowl for 1/2 hour.
3. Heat oil in a pan at medium high temperature.
4. Fry chicken for 2 to 3 minutes or until chicken is golden brown.
5. Remove chicken and drain excess oil on paper towels.
6. Pour lemon chicken sauce* on top of chicken and serve.

* See page 107 for the lemon chicken sauce recipe.

Always Worth the Trip to Eat at L & L

"We missss you guys here!!!!" So we would like to say, "Open up one close to Wellington, Ohio." Dennis, Hawaii Kai

Mochiko Chicken

Serves 5 to 6 people

Ingredients

- 2 to 2-1/2 pounds of boneless chicken thighs (cut into 2 inches by 1 inch)
- 1/3 cup of mochiko flour
- 1/3 cup of corn starch
- 1/3 cup of soy sauce
- 1/3 cup of sugar
- 1 teaspoon of garlic (minced)
- 1/2 teaspoon of salt
- 2 eggs (beaten)
- 1/4 cup of green onion (diced)
- 1 teaspoon of ginger (grated)
- Vegetable oil

Steps

1. Combine and mix ingredients except vegetable oil in a bowl.
2. Place bowl in the refrigerator overnight.
3. Heat pan with vegetable oil at medium high temperature.
4. Fry chicken until it is golden brown or done.
5. Remove chicken and place it on paper towel to remove excess oil before serving.

Dumb Question

"Aloha! It is an amazing feeling walking into a restaurant and feeling you are at home (in the islands). The music, smell and of course the food and Hawaiian Sun at Renton L & L." Anthony, Issaquah

Chicken Laulau

Serves 3 to 4 people

Ingredients

- 1/2 butterfish
- 1-1/2 pounds of chicken thighs
- Hawaiian salt or plain salt
- 1 pound taro leaves
- 8 to 10 ti leaves

Steps

1. Season chicken thighs and butterfish with Hawaiian salt.
2. Divide chicken thighs and butterfish into 8 to 10 parts.
3. Wrap a piece of chicken thigh and butterfish with taro leaves.
4. Place each wrap with a set of ti leaves.
5. Tie the end of the ti leaves with string.
6. Place wrapped laulau in a large steamer.
7. Cover steamer and steam for 4 hours or more.
8. Remove laulau.
9. Carefully unwrap laulau and serve.

Healthy or Regular Hawaiian BBQ

"I LOVE L & L because of the big portions for low price! Always hot and fresh off the grill at the counter always knows what I want!" Henry, Hawaii Loa Ridge

Chicken Long Rice

Serves 6 to 7 people

Ingredients

- 2 pounds of skinless chicken thighs
- Hawaiian salt or plain salt
- 10 ounces of "long rice" noodles (aka cellophane noodles or sai fun)
- 2 garlic cloves (minced or crushed)
- 2 tablespoons of fresh minced ginger
- 2 tablespoons of vegetable oil
- 2 (14.5 ounce) cans of chicken broth
- Dash of pepper
- 2 to 4 green onions (chopped)

Steps

1. Cut chicken thighs into small pieces or strips and sprinkle with Hawaiian salt.
2. Soak long rice in cold water for 30 minutes and cut into smaller pieces.
3. Sauté garlic and ginger.
4. Add chicken and cook until the chicken is brown.
5. Add 2 cans of chicken broth and bring to a boil.
6. Turn to low heat and cook for 40 to 50 minutes.
7. Add the rest of the ingredients and cook for another 3 to 5 minutes.
8. Be careful not to overcook the long rice.
9. Garnish with green onions.

Free Range Chicken Special Diet

"I love your fresh chicken and absolutely love the katsu sauce, yummy! Please can you have a restaurant in San Antonio? I miss your ono food. Da Best!" Yanny, San Antonio

Shoyu Chicken

Serves 4 to 5 people

Ingredients

- 2 to 3 cloves of garlic
- 1 small piece of ginger
- 2/3 cup of soy sauce
- 1/3 cup of sugar
- 1-1/2 cup of water
- 3 to 4 pounds of chicken thighs

Steps

1. Combine all ingredients except chicken thighs in a pot.
2. Cook for about 1 to 2 minutes.
3. Add chicken thighs and bring to a boil.
4. Turn down heat and simmer for 30 to 40 minutes or until chicken is tender.

* In Hawaii, soy sauce is known as shoyu sauce. For best tasting shoyu chicken, use Yamasa soy sauce.

Don't Ask, Don't Tell

"I can go to L & L to my neighborhood outside of Denver! No joke! Grind time!! Hawaiian Sun and plate lunch! Grind time!" Sai, Aurora

Chicken Luau

Serves 6 to 8 people

Ingredients

- 2 pounds of taro leaves
- 2 cups of water
- 3 to 4 bone-in chicken thighs
- Vegetable oil
- 2 cups of coconut milk
- 1 teaspoon of Hawaiian salt or plain salt

Steps

1. Clean taro leaves thoroughly and discard stems (wear gloves to clean).
2. Put taro leaves into a pot of water.
3. Cook for 1 to 2 hours or until the taro leaves reach a desired consistency (very soft).
4. Remove bone from chicken thighs and cut into small pieces.
5. Sauté chicken with vegetable oil for about 5 minutes or until it is brown.
6. Drain taro leaves and stir the remaining ingredients into pan.
7. Cook in low heat until it is done.

Saturday Night Live at the Cockfight

" We miss L & L. We all eat it every day almost in Hawaii when we lived there in Schofield Barracks. The discount coupons were great." Jennifer, Kaneohe

Hawaiian Huli Huli Chicken

Serves 8 to 10 people

Ingredients

- 1/2 tablespoon of sesame oil
- 1/3 cup of ketchup
- 1/3 cup of soy sauce
- 1 /2 cup of brown sugar
- 3 tablespoons sherry
- 1 piece of ginger (crushed)
- 1 to 2 pieces of garlic (crushed)
- 4 to 5 pounds of chicken pieces

Steps

1. Combine all ingredients except chicken in a bowl.
2. Marinate the chicken in the mixture for 1 hour.
3. Cook over charcoal grill.
4. Take turn to brush chicken on each side with marinade until cooked.
5. Remove chicken and serve hot.

The Loser is One Tough Chicken

"I love your chicken katsu and bbq chicken. They are always freshly cooked to order and taste sooo ono." Jim, Lafayette

Chicken Adobo

Serves 4 to 6 people

Ingredients

- 1 teaspoon of vegetable oil
- 1 whole garlic (chopped and smashed)
- Salt (divided use)
- 1 whole chicken (cut into 8 to 10 pieces)
- 1 cup of soy sauce
- 1 cup of white vinegar
- 1 tablespoons of peppercorns (crushed)
- 3 bay leaves

Steps

1. Heat oil and sauté garlic to golden brown in a pot.
2. Add lightly salted chicken into pot until it is tender.
3. Combine and stir soy sauce, vinegar, peppercorns, bay leaves into pot.
4. Bring it to a boil at a low heat.
5. Simmer for 25 to 30 minutes until the liquid has evaporated.
6. Add salt for taste and stir occasionally.
7. Serve with hot rice.

Hawaii's New Illegal Immigrants - Coqui Frogs

"You guys are the best!!! I love it all. Great food, good looking girls (most of the time), and great employees. Keep up the great Ohana."
Gerry, Manoa

Chinese Chicken Salad

Serves 5 to 6 people

Ingredients

- 1/4 cup of sugar
- 1/3 cup of vinegar
- 1 teaspoon of Hawaiian salt
- 1/2 teaspoon of pepper
- 1 head lettuce (shredded)
- 2 to 3 stalks of green onion (diced)
- 2 to 3 cups of slivered celery
- 1/8 tablespoon of sesame oil
- 1/2 cup of salad oil
- 2 to 3 meaty chicken breasts (cooked and shredded)
- 2 bunches of Chinese parsley (chopped)
- 1/2 cup of peanuts (chopped)
- 6 ounces of wonton chips

Steps

1. Combine sugar, vinegar, oil, Hawaiian salt, and pepper in a salad bowl to make dressing.
2. Combine lettuce, green onion, celery, sesame and salad oil, shredded chicken, and Chinese parsley in the salad bowl.
3. When you are ready to serve, pour dressing over salad and toss gently.
4. Garnish with peanuts and wonton chips.

David & Goliath

"I usually go to L & L after doing weight training for the real chicken katsu plate…Ono Ono." Stanfield, Roseville

Hamburger Patties

Makes about 10 patties

Ingredients

- 2 pounds of ground hamburger meat
- 1 cup of bread crumbs
- 1 small onion (chopped)
- 1 egg
- 1 teaspoon of salt
- 1 teaspoon of black pepper
- 1 tablespoon of Worcestershire sauce
- Vegetable oil

Steps

1. Combine and mix the ingredients in a bowl.
2. Make about 10 patties.
3. Heat pan with vegetable oil.
4. Cook for about 2 to 3 minutes on each side.

Hawaii's Favorite Food Has A Funny Meaning

"I am craving for Loco Moco with spam and rice wrapped around with seaweed. Congratulations on the success of your company."
Juncay, Fremont

Loco Moco

One Serving

Ingredients

- 2 hamburger patties *[1]
- 1 cup gravy *[2]
- 1 cup of steam rice
- 2 eggs (sunny side up, over easy or scrambled)

Steps

1. Heat pan to medium high temperature.
2. Grill hamburger patties to your satisfaction.
3. Scoop rice onto plate.
4. Place hamburger patties on top.
5. Place eggs on top of the hamburger patties.
6. Pour gravy on top of the eggs.

*[1] See page 37 for the hamburger patties recipe

*[2] See page 113 for the brown gravy recipe

Asking for Trouble in Paradise

"I LOVE THIS PLACE. NO SHIRT AND NO SHOES but plenty Aloha spirit at Provo. I can jump straight into the surf." Spencer, Salt Lake City

Beef Stew

Serves 5 to 7 people

Ingredients

- 2 to 3 teaspoons of Hawaiian salt
- 1 teaspoon of white pepper
- Vegetable oil
- 2 pounds of beef (chuck roast)
- 1 quart of beef broth
- 1 medium onion (chopped)
- 2 stalks of celery (chopped)
- 1 teaspoon of garlic (minced)
- 2 to 3 teaspoons of sugar
- 1/4 cup of Worcestershire sauce
- 1 cup of ketchup
- 1/4 cup tomato paste
- 3 bay leaves
- 2 potatoes (cut into 1 inch cubes)
- 2 carrots (cut into 1 inch cubes)
- 1/4 cup flour
- 1/4 cup water

Steps

1. Sprinkle salt and pepper on meat.
2. Heat pot with oil and lightly sauté meat until brown on both sides
3. Pour broth into a pot and bring to a boil. Remove excess scum that floats to the top of the pot.
4. Add remaining ingredients except carrots and potatoes, then bring to a boil.
5. Simmer for 40 to 50 minutes until meat is tender.
6. Add carrots and simmer for 4 to 5 minutes.
7. Add potatoes and simmer for another 10 to 12 minutes.
8. Mix flour and water then pour into the pot to finish the stew.

Hawaiian Lava Rocks Make Hot Curry

“DROOOLLLLL!! I miss Hawaii. Born and RAISED….THANK GOD you guys help me survive in the mainland!” Jim, Happy Valley

Beef Curry

Serves 5 to 7 people

Ingredients

- 1/4 cup flour
- 1/4 cup water
- 2 to 3 teaspoons of Hawaiian salt
- 1 teaspoon of white pepper
- Vegetable oil
- 2 pounds of chuck roast beef (cut into 1 inch cubes)
- 1 quart of beef broth
- 1 medium onion (chopped)
- 2 stalks of celery (chopped)
- 3 bay leaves
- 1 cup of cabbage (chopped)
- 3 tablespoon of curry powder
- 1 teaspoon of minced garlic
- 2 tablespoon of sugar
- 2 potatoes (cut into 1 inch cubes)
- 2 carrots (cut into 1 inch cubes)

Steps

1. Mix flour and water to make roux.
2. Sprinkle salt and pepper on meat.
3. Heat pot with oil and sauté meat until brown on both sides.
4. Pour beef broth into pot and bring to a boil. Remove excess scum that floats to the top of the pot.
5. Add remaining ingredients except potatoes and carrots and bring to a boil.
6. Simmer for 40 minutes or until meat is tender.
7. Add carrots and cook for 4 to 6 minutes.
8. Add potatoes and cook for 10 to 12 minutes.
9. Pour roux into pot and finish cooking.

Kobe Beef Needs Daily Massage & Beer

"Lunch Break: A Trip to Hawaii Without Leaving NYC By Eating at L & L." Chuck, Tokyo

Teriyaki Beef

Serves 5 to 6 people

Ingredients

- 2 to 2-1/2 pounds chuck roast (sliced)
- 1 quart of teriyaki sauce*
- Dash of sesame oil

Steps

1. Combine and mix ingredients in a pot for 2 hours prior to cooking.
2. Heat pan to medium heat with sesame oil.
3. Cook beef until done.

* See page 105 for the teriyaki sauce recipe.

Eddie Road

"You are killing me!! I would love some katsu and that awesome macaroni salad!!!! Come to the Midwest soon?? Maybe Omaha?????" Bill, Las Vegas

Hawaiian Barbecue Short Ribs

Serves 5 to 6 people

Ingredients

- 2 to 2-1/2 pounds chuck roast (sliced)
- 1 quart of teriyaki sauce*
- 1/3 green onion (diced)
- Dash of sesame oil

Steps

1. Combine and mix ingredients in a pot for 2 hours prior to cooking.
2. Heat pan to medium high temperature.
3. Put short ribs in pan and fry for 2 to 3 minutes each side.

* See page 105 for the teriyaki sauce recipe.

Hot Big Island Real Estate

"The lava at the Big Island is great but the plate lunches at L & L is better." Wesley, Kona

Chili

Serves 4 to 5 people

Ingredients

- 1/4 cup flour
- 1/4 cup water
- Vegetable oil
- 1 teaspoon of garlic (minced)
- 2 stalk of celery (diced)
- 1/2 medium onion (minced)
- 1 green bell pepper (diced)
- 1 pound ground hamburger meat
- 2 cups of beef broth
- 2 teaspoons of chili powder
- 1/2 teaspoon of white pepper
- 1 teaspoon of salt
- 1 teaspoon of sugar
- 1/3 cup of ketchup
- 1 tablespoon of tomato paste
- 1 can 14 oz. of kidney beans (rinsed and drained)
- Tabasco sauce for taste

Steps

1. Mix flour and water in a cup to make roux.
2. Heat pan with vegetable oil and add garlic.
3. Brown the vegetables.
4. Add brown meat to vegetables.
5. Add broth and the remaining ingredients.
6. Bring to boil and slowly stir in the roux.
7. Cook for 15 to 20 minutes and serve on hot rice.

Miss Rat Hates L & L

"Ashton Kutcher wearing L & L t-shirt on USA Weekend Magazine. He must like da kine grind." Ben, Kalihi

Meat Jun

Serves 2 to 3 people

Ingredients

- 1 pound of sirloin tip or flank steak (thinly sliced)
- 1/2 cup of flour
- 3 eggs (beaten and place in a cup)
- 2 tablespoons of vegetable oil

Steps

1. Soak the meat in the meat jun sauce* for 1 hour.
2. Dredge meat in flour and dip in beaten eggs.
3. Fry in hot oil until both sides of the meat are golden brown.
4. Place the meat on paper towels to drain off excess oil.

* See page 109 for meat jun sauce recipe.

Keep Praying - L & L Will Open in your Area Soon

"Santa Cruz is begging for an L & L. We need a lil aloha. After a good surf….stoke the masses on some chicken katsu." Willie W., San Jose

Pipikaula

Serves 5 to 8 people

Ingredients

- 4 pounds of flank steak
- 2 cups of soy sauce
- 2 tablespoons of Hawaiian salt
- 2 tablespoons of sugar
- 1/4 teaspoon of pepper
- 1 small piece of ginger (minced)
- 2 Hawaiian red peppers (crushed)
- 2 cloves of garlic (minced)

Steps

1. Trim fat from flank steak and cut meat into long strips of about 2 inches wide.
2. Combine ingredients in large bowl for 24 hours in the refrigerator.
3. Stir meat several times within the 24 hours.
4. Preheat oven at 200 degrees.
5. Drain meat and arrange on cooling racks set on baking sheets.
6. Dry meat in oven for 6 to 7 hours or until the texture of the meat has the consistency of beef jerky.
7. Store meat in refrigerator for 5 to 6 days or freeze for up to 8 months.
8. Slice diagonally and heat before serving.

Wrong Place, Wrong Time

"I almost lost my job because I had to have my L & L fix for lunch. Went way over my allotted 1 hour break.... But it is worth every bite!" Teresa, Honolulu

Hawaiian Barbecue Pork Chops

Serves 4 to 5 people

Ingredients

- 2 pounds of pork chops (about 4 ounces each)
- 1 quart of teriyaki sauce*
- 1 tablespoon sesame oil
- 1 tablespoon vegetable oil

Steps

1. Combine all ingredients except vegetable oil and marinade for 2 hours.
2. Heat pan at medium heat with vegetable oil.
3. Fry meat for 2 to 3 minutes on each side.

* See page 105 for the teriyaki sauce recipe.

Dancing Queens

"Spam musubi and plate lunch….These are feel-good foods @ L & L Hawaiian BBQ – guarantee to please." Karen, Honolulu

Kalua Pork

Serves 5 to 6 people

Ingredients

- 2 pounds of pork butt (cut into 1-1/2 inches cubes)
- 3 bay leaves
- 2 quarts of beef broth
- 2 tablespoons of salt
- 1/2 teaspoon of garlic powder
- 1/2 teaspoon of white pepper
- 1 medium onion (chopped)
- 1/4 bunch celery
- 1/2 cup of liquid smoke

Steps

1. Combine all ingredients in a pot and bring to a boil.
2. Remove excess scum and fat.
3. Simmer for 2-1/2 hours or until the pork is ready for shredding.
4. Shred pork with a tong and serve.

Free Loading Grandmother

"We love your Musubi Eating contest. Please, please… do it again."
Nancy, Providence

SPAM Musubi

One Serving

Ingredients

- Vegetable oil
- 3/4 cup of steam rice
- 1 teaspoon of barbecue sauce*
- 1 piece of Spam (1 can sliced and divided into 8 pieces)
- 1/2 sheet of nori (seaweed wrap)

Steps

1. Heat pan with oil and lightly pan fry Spam.
2. Put rice into a musubi mold.
3. Put barbecue sauce on top of rice.
4. Place Spam on top of rice.
5. Wrap nori around rice and serve.

* See page 103 for the Hawaiian barbecue sauce recipe.

Beach Bum

"Haleiwa has the BEST garlic shrimp I have ever had and delicious mac salad and rice. I miss it now that I am back in the mainland."
Peter, Fuzhou

Pork Lumpia

Serves 5 to 8 people

Ingredients

- Vegetable oil (1 quart, 1 teaspoon)
- 1 pound of ground pork
- 2 cloves garlic (crushed)
- 1/2 cup onion (sliced)
- 1/2 cup green onion
- 1/4 cup carrot (julienned)
- 2 packages of bean sprouts
- 1/4 teaspoon of pepper
- 1/4 cup of water
- 2 tablespoons of flour
- 40 lumpia wrappers
- Salt

Steps

1. Heat about one teaspoon of oil in large pan and sauté pork until barely done.
2. Remove pork and drain skillet.
3. Sauté garlic and onion for 1 minute.
4. Add vegetables and seasoning and cook for 2 minutes, place in a large bowl to cool.
5. Make paste by combing water with flour.
6. Place 2 to 3 tablespoons of fillings on a wrapper.
7. Fold nearest wedge over fillings.
8. Roll wrappers with open edges.
9. Fold and seal edges with paste.
10. Heat about one quart of vegetable oil in the pan and fry lumpia until both sides are golden brown.
11. Soak up excess oil with paper towels and serve.

Pigs are Always Welcome to the Luau

"I am a huge fan of L & L. I've tried other Hawaiian food but never again will I do it cuz it just upsets me that no other Hawaiian bbq food is as good as L & L." Gary, Monterey Park

Pork Adobo

Serves 4 to 6 people

Ingredients

- Vegetable oil (1 quart, 1 teaspoon)
- 2 to 3 pounds of pork belly (cut into 1-inch pieces)
- 1 cup of soy sauce
- 1 cup of white vinegar
- 2 tablespoons of peppercorns (crushed)
- 3 bay leaves
- 1 small garlic (chopped and smashed)
- 1 teaspoon of vegetable oil
- Salt

Steps

1. Combine pork belly, soy sauce, and garlic and marinate for 2 hours.
2. Combine and stir the remaining ingredients into a pot.
3. Bring it to a boil at low heat and simmer for 35 to 45 minutes or until pork is tender.
4. Add salt for taste and stir occasionally.
5. Serve hot with rice.

Economics 101: Supply & Demand

"Mahalo for this place at Fulton Street, NYC……I got a feeling as if I was in the islands myself with the decorations, music, and Keoki's laulau with kalua pork." Bryan, Amherst

Pork Laulau

Serves 3 to 4 people

Ingredients

- 1/2 butterfish
- 1 pound of pork butt (cut into 8 to 10 cubes)
- Hawaiian salt or plain salt
- 8 to 10 ti leaves
- 1 pound of taro leaves

Steps

1. Season butterfish and pork with Hawaiian salt.
2. Divide pork and butterfish into 8 to 10 parts. Rub pork with salt.
3. Wrap a piece of pork and butterfish with taro leaves.
4. Place each wrap with a set of ti leaves.
5. Tie the end of the ti leaves with string.
6. Place wrapped laulau in a large steamer.
7. Cover steamer and steam for 4 hours or more.
8. Remove laulau.
9. Carefully unwrap laulau and serve.

Miss Laulau Before Her Hot Steam Bath

"Dear L & L, Please open a branch of your awesome restaurant in Chicago!!! I tried the Loco Moco for the first time in Las Vegas and I've been wanting to have craving for it again." Ben, Chicago

Quick Serving Laulau

Serves 3 to 4 people

Keoki's Laulau is available in most Asian supermarkets on the West Coast or at any L & L Hawaiian Barbecue location. The laulau usually comes in a package of three. If you are unable to buy laulau in your area, please contact:

L & L Hawaiian Barbecue
931 University Avenue
Honolulu, Hawaii 96826
Phone: 808-951-9888
Email: info@hawaiianbarbecue.com
Website: www.hawaiianbarbecue.com

Keoki's Laulau
966 Robello Lane
Honolulu, Hawaii 96817
Phone: 808-832-9500

Steps

1. Remove laulau from the freezer. Unwrap plastic package.
2. Place in a steamer.
3. Boil water and steam for at least 40 to 50 minutes.
4. Remove laulau from the steamer.
5. Carefully unwrap laulau leaves and serve.

Hilo has Sweet Longan (Dragon Eyes)

"I love L & L Hawaiian food! And now there's healthy choices! Yes! I'm on a diet so that works out perfectly. Try the garlic shrimp." Ping, Elk Grove

Deep Fried Shrimp

Serves 4 to 5 people

Ingredients

- 1 cup of flour
- 1 cup of corn starch
- 1 teaspoon of salt
- 1/2 teaspoon of pepper
- 1/2 teaspoon of garlic powder
- 1 egg
- 1 tablespoon of salad oil
- 1-1/2 cup of water
- 1 pound of shrimp (butterfly)
- 3 cups of panko (Japanese bread crumbs)*
- Vegetable oil

Steps

1. Combine all the ingredients except panko, shrimps and vegetable oil to make the batter.
2. Dip the shrimp into batter.
3. Bread battered shrimp with panko.
4. Heat oil in a pan and fry until the shrimp is golden brown.

* For best-tasting deep fried shrimp, use Upper Crust panko.

Catch of the Day

"There was something about the katsu sauce in Kaneohe that I have never been able to duplicate! It is different from other L & Ls."
Howard, Kaneohe

Deep Fried Shrimp

Serves 4 to 6 people

Ingredients

- 2 pounds of mahi mahi (sliced into 3-ounce pieces)
- 2 eggs
- 1 cup of corn starch
- 1/2 cup of water
- 1 teaspoon white pepper
- 1 teaspoon of sesame oil
- 1 teaspoon of garlic powder
- 2 cups of chicken fry mix
- Vegetable oil

Steps

1. Combine ingredients except chicken fry mix and vegetable oil to make the batter.
2. Dip mahi mahi into batter and coat with chicken fry mix.
3. Heat pan at medium high temperature with vegetable oil.
4. Deep fry until golden brown.

Early Bird Special

"Spam Musubi Tuesday in L & L Fullerton. The best I ever eaten.! Oh did I mention they're 99 cents!?" Annie, Diamond Bar

Fried Ahi

Serves 4 to 6 people

Ingredients

- 2 pounds of ahi (sliced into 3-ounce pieces)
- 2 eggs
- 1 cup of corn starch
- 1/2 cup of water
- 1 teaspoon of white pepper
- 1 teaspoon of sesame oil
- 1 teaspoon of garlic powder
- 2 cups of McCormick chicken fry mix
- Vegetable oil

Steps

1. Combine ingredients except chicken fry mix and vegetable oil to make the batter.
2. Dip ahi into the batter and coat with chicken fry mix.
3. Heat pan at medium high temperature with vegetable oil.
4. Fry fish until golden brown.

Da Best Garlic Shrimp

"Spam Musubi Tuesday in L & L Fullerton. The best I ever eaten.! Oh did I mention they're 99 cents!?" Annie, Diamond Bar

Garlic Shrimp

Serves 3 to 4 people

Ingredients

- 1/2 teaspoon of salt
- 1/2 teaspoon of white pepper
- 1 pound shrimp size 26-30 (cleaned and deveined)
- 1/2 cup of cornstarch
- 3 cups of vegetable oil
- 1/2 cup of garlic (minced)
- 1/2 cup of butter
- 1/2 cup of green onion (diced)

Steps

1. Season the shrimp with salt, white pepper.
2. Coat shrimp with cornstarch.
3. Heat pan with vegetable oil at medium high temperature.
4. Fry shrimp in small batches.
5. Heat another pan with vegetable oil at medium high temperature.
6. Sauté garlic to golden brown.
7. Add butter, green onions, and later the shrimp.
8. Mix all the ingredients and serve.

Slow Cookers

"Miss you guys out here in South Carolina. I use to eat lunch with you 4-5 times in National City. The mix bbq and macaroni made with Best Foods mayo…ono." Alec, Thousand Oaks

Shrimp Tempura

Serves 3 to 4 people

Ingredients

- 10 to 12 large shrimps (butterfly)
- 1 egg
- 1 cup of ice water
- 1 cup of flour
- Vegetable oil for deep-frying

Steps

1. Remove heads and shell except tails.
2. Devein the shrimps.
3. Dry shrimps on paper towel.
4. Beat the egg in a small bowl.
5. Add ice water in the bowl.
6. Combine and mix in the flour.
7. Heat pan with oil at medium high temperature.
8. Dust the shrimps with flour.
9. Hold shrimps by the tails and dip into the batter.
10. Deep fry until the shrimps are crisp

Waikiki Aquarium Fish Market

"I just had a garlic mahi mahi plate for dinner the other night (Keeaumoku).. it was delicious. YUMMY food!!!!!!!!!!!!!!!!" Sole, Waikiki

Lomi Salmon

Serves 6 to 8 people

Ingredients

- 1 pound salmon (salted)
- 3 to 4 tomatoes (diced)
- 2 medium onions (diced)
- 3 to 4 green onions (thinly sliced)
- Hawaiian salt or plain salt

Steps

1. Soak the salted salmon in cold water for 1 to 2 hours.
2. Change the water a couple of times, each time add ice cubes.
3. Remove salted salmon skin and bone.
4. Cut salted salmon into small cubes.
5. Combine all ingredients and mix with your fingers (lomi).
6. Cover bowl and chill for 2 to 3 hours.
7. Serve chilled.

Cutting Cost in a Recession - Hawaiian Style

"Thanks Fresno L & L. Had your bbq chicken, bbq beef, white rice and mac salad for my birthday Luau today – it was the bomb!! Your L & L employees were great." Josie, Fresno

Squid Luau

Serves 6 to 8 people

Ingredients

- 2 pounds of taro leaves
- 2 cups of water
- 2 cups of coconut milk
- 1 teaspoon of Hawaiian salt
- 1 to 2 pounds of squid

Steps

1. Clean taro leaves thoroughly and discard stems (wear gloves to clean).
2. Put taro leaves into a pot with water.
3. Cook for 1 to 2 hours or until the taro leaves reach a desired consistency (very soft).
4. Clean squid and cut into rings.
5. Drain taro leaves and stir the remaining ingredients into pan.
6. Cook in low heat until it is done.

Will Work for Plate Lunch

"Hey…I saw Janet Jackson eating at L & L in Liliha Street. The pop diva grinds on plate lunch. She no like take picture." Keith, Kaimuki

Vegetable Lumpia

Serves 5 to 8 people

Ingredients

- 2 cloves of garlic (crushed)
- 1/2 cup of onion (sliced)
- 1/4 cup of carrot (julienned)
- 2 packages of bean sprouts
- 1/2 cup of green onion (cut into small pieces)
- 1 teaspoon of salt
- 1/4 teaspoon of pepper
- 1/4 cup of water
- 2 tablespoons of flour
- 40 lumpia wrappers
- Vegetable oil

Steps

1. Sauté garlic and onion for 1 minute.
2. Add vegetables and seasoning and cook for another 2 minutes.
3. Place in a large bowl to cool.
4. Make paste by combing water with flour.
5. Place 2 to 3 tablespoons of fillings on a wrapper.
6. Fold nearest wedge over fillings.
7. Roll wrappers with open edges.
8. Fold and seal edges with paste.
9. Heat vegetable oil in the pan and fry lumpia until both sides are golden brown.
10. Soak up excess oil with paper towels and serve.

Da Bosses Giving Back

"Thank you for the 76 cents promotion. It really helps my family for a great ono meal. Mahalo!" Henry, Mapunapuna

Kim Chee

Serves 4 to 5 people

Ingredients

- 1 large Chinese cabbage
- 1 gallon of water
- 1/2 cup of salt
- 1 teaspoon of sugar
- 1/3 cup of chili paste
- 1 medium daikon (grated)
- 1 small clove of garlic (finely minced)
- 1 small piece of ginger (minced)
- 1/2 cup of green onion (chopped)

Steps

1. Cut cabbage into 3-inch length.
2. Put cabbage in salted water for 2 hours in a pot and make sure the cabbage is submerged.
3. Combine the remaining ingredients in a bowl.
4. Drain and rinse the cabbage and squeeze out the excess water.
5. Combine the cabbage with all other ingredients in a large glass jar.
6. Cover the glass jar tightly.
7. Leave mixture in a cool place for 1 to 2 days and until bubbling a bit inside the glass jar.
8. Refrigerate the glass jar for 3 to 4 days before serving.

All We Want for Christmas

"I would fly to the moon on a bunch of balloons to get to L & L and then surf on some stars until I get to Mars for chicken katsu."
Caroline, Waipahu

Vegetable Saimin

One Serving

Ingredients

- 6 cups of water
- 3 to 4 ounces of saimin noodles*
- Vegetable oil
- 1 teaspoon of green onion (diced)
- Vegetables (bean sprouts, Chinese cabbage, etc. cut into small pieces)
- 2 teaspoons of saimin soup base

Steps

1. Put 4 cups of water into pot and bring it to a boil.
2. Put loose noodles into boiling water for 1 minute.
3. Remove noodles and strain water.
4. Wash noodles in cold water.
5. Stir fried vegetables with oil.
6. Boil 2 cups of water.
7. Add and stir soup base.
8. Add noodles and vegetables to serve.

* For best tasting saimin, use Sun Noodle's products at 1933 Colburn Street, Honolulu, Hawaii 96819, telephone: 808-841-5808 or www.sunnoodle.com.

Kalua Pork Plate Lunch To Go

"THANK YOU ...THANK YOU ...THANK YOU... FOR YOUR HAPPY VALLEY ARIZONA L & L....IT'S ALWAYS NICE TO HAVE A TASTE OF HOME WHEN YOU ARE SO FAR AWAY....THANK YOU." Jun, Milpitas

Vegetable Tempura

Serves 3 to 4 people

Ingredients

- 1 egg
- 1 cup of ice water
- 1 cup of flour plus more for dusting
- Vegetable oil
- Sweet potatoes (sliced)
- Eggplant (sliced)
- Carrots (sliced)

Steps

1. Beat egg in a small bowl.
2. Add ice water in the bowl.
3. Combine and mix in the flour.
4. Heat pan with oil at medium high temperature.
5. Dust the vegetables with flour.
6. Dip into the batter.
7. Deep-fry until the vegetables are crisp.

Cheap Hawaiian Date

"I love L & L Hawaiian Barbecue! I stopped tonight for my birthday on my way home to bring some home! Only thing I wanted for my special day." Elaine, Honolulu

Healthy Hawaiian Barbecue Plates

Contrary to the rumor that I do not eat at L & L, I love my Hawaiian barbecue, especially the skinless barbecue chicken plate with curry on top of the macaroni salad and rice. However, my wife Elaine, a yoga enthusiast, preferred vegetarian food and refused to eat at L & L.

Fifteen years ago, I asked our executive chef, Raymond Cheng, to create the first healthy Hawaiian barbecue plate for my wife. It is quite simple to make the healthy Hawaiian barbecue. The first ingredient is brown rice. Next, add a serving of tossed green salad with low fat dressing. Finally, add a small portion of protein such as skinless BBQ chicken, garlic shrimp, garlic mahi mahi, etc. Garnish with fresh fruits such as grapes or pineapple and the delicious L & L Healthy Hawaiian Barbecue plate is complete.

We tried to market the first healthy Hawaiian barbecue plate in San Francisco, and the response was great. Then we gradually introduced it to other West Coast cities. Eventually, the healthy plate came home to Hawaii. Now, it is standard on all our menus in the L & L Hawaiian Barbecue chain.

Nowadays, my wife, Elaine has no excuse not to eat at L & L. On our anniversary, I usually take my wife to enjoy a candle light dinner on the beach, watch the sunset on the horizon and eat our favorite L & L Hawaiian Barbecue Healthy plates.

Quick Switch

"I need plenty meat. I'm glad there is one L & L Hawaiian Barbecue in America Samoa. Bring me the big MATAI PLATE." Itula, American Samoa

Skinless Hawaiian Barbecue Chicken Healthy Plate

Serves 3 to 4 people

Ingredients

- 1 scoop of brown rice
- 1 cup of tossed green salad
- 3 slices of cucumber
- 2 tomato wedges
- 1 tablespoon of kidney beans
- 1 piece of Hawaiian barbecue chicken*

Steps

1. Arrange rice and vegetables in a nice presentation.
2. Cut chicken into small pieces and place on top of salad.
3. Serve with your favorite low fat dressing.

* You may substitute the Hawaiian barbecue chicken with garlic shrimp, Hawaiian barbecue beef, grilled ahi, grilled salmon, etc.

Oxtail Soup

"Sittin' here in Brooklyn, NY, noshin' on da laulau from L & L!"
David, Rutgers University

Hawaiian Oxtail Soup

Serves 5 to 6 people

Ingredients

- 2 pieces of Chinese dried tangerine peel
- 4 to 5 pounds of oxtails (cut into pieces)
- 2 cans of beef broth
- 2 cans of chicken broth
- 3 carrots (cut into small pieces)
- 1 pound of raw peanuts
- 6 Chinese dried red dates
- 10 slices of Chinese mustard cabbage
- 1 piece of fresh ginger (sliced)
- Salt
- 1 bunch of Chinese parsley (chopped)
- Fresh ground ginger and soy sauce (dipping sauce)

Steps

1. Soak dried tangerine peel for 10 minutes to remove membrane.
2. Meanwhile, parboil the oxtails in a pot for 30 minutes.
3. Rinse the oxtails in fresh water and drain.
4. Trim off the fat from the oxtails.
5. Combine with beef broth, chicken broth, 12 to 15 cups of water, carrots, raw peanuts, dates, dried tangerine peel, and fresh ginger.
6. Bring to a boil and simmer for 1-1/2 to 2 hours.
7. Add Chinese cabbage and cook for another five minutes.
8. Add salt to taste and Chinese parsley for decoration.
9. Dip oxtails into ground ginger soy sauce and serve with rice.

Da Fabulous Hawaiian Cockroach

"Awesome Restaurant!!! Brings us "local" folks on the mainland back to the islands with some ono grinds. We're on a family vacation and we're making a stop or two to L & L. I'm soooo excited!!" Arsen, Northridge

Portuguese Bean Soup

Serves 8 to 10 people

Ingredients

- 2 to 3 medium sized smoked ham hocks or ham shanks
- 3 cans of chicken broth
- 1 quart of water
- 1 medium onion (chopped)
- 1 can tomato paste (16 ounce)
- 1 cup of celery (diced)
- 2 cans of kidney beans
- 1 clove of garlic (smashed)
- 1 teaspoon of pepper
- 1/2 pound of uncooked elbow macaroni
- 2 bay leaves
- 3 to 4 cups of cabbage (chopped)
- 4 carrots (diced)
- 4 potatoes (cut into 1/2 to 1 inch cubes)
- 1 pound of Portuguese sausage (cut into halves and sliced)

Steps

1. Put ham hock and chicken broth in a large pot.
2. Add water and boil for 1 to 2 hours or until tender.
3. Skim off the fat from the pot.
4. Add remaining ingredients and cook until the vegetables are tender.

Arch Rivalry

"I just had your platter and I'm about to devour your spam rice seaweed brick thing. The gods didn't eat this well in Mt. Olympus."
Justin, Portland

Katsu Sauce

Serves 5 to 6 people

Ingredients

- 2 tablespoons of corn starch
- 2 tablespoons of water
- 1 cup of ketchup
- 2-1/2 cups of water
- 1/2 cup of sugar
- 1/2 cup of Worcestershire sauce
- 1/2 teaspoon of white pepper
- 1/2 teaspoon of garlic powder
- 2 tablespoons of soy sauce

Steps

1. Combine and mix corn starch and water to make roux.
2. Combine ingredients except roux in a pot and bring to a boil.
3. Slowly stir roux into pot.
4. Let it cool and serve.

Paradise Found

"Thank You, Thank You!! I grew up as the only haole in my school in Nanakuli and have been suffering from withdrawal for saimin for years until I came across the L & L in Connecticut." Alfredo, Maui

Tartar Sauce

Serves 5 to 6 people

Ingredients

- 2 cups of mayonnaise*
- 1/4 cup of relish
- 1/2 lemon juice

Steps

1. Combine and mix all ingredients together.
2. Chill and serve.

* For best tasting tartar sauce, use Best Foods or Hellmann's mayonnaise.

How to Be First in Line

"I love your 76 cents plate lunch even if I had to wait 3 hours for an ono chicken katsu." Edna, Salt Lake

Hawaiian Barbecue Sauce

Serves 5 to 6 people

Ingredients

- 2 tablespoons of flour
- 2 tablespoons of water
- 1 cup of water
- 1 cup of soy sauce*
- 1/2 teaspoon of black pepper
- 1/2 teaspoon garlic powder
- 3/4 cup of sugar

Steps

1. Combine and mix cornstarch and water to make roux.
2. Combine ingredients except roux in a pot and bring to boil.
3. Slowly stir in roux and bring to a boil again.

* In Hawaii, soy sauce is known as shoyu sauce. For best tasting shoyu chicken, use Yamasa soy sauce.

Jack & the Beanstalk

"Awesome food. Big portions. Delicious. Ono Ono." John, Hayward

Teriyaki Sauce

Serves 5 to 6 people

Ingredients

- 2-1/2 cups of water
- 1/2 pound of sugar
- 1 cup of soy sauce*
- 1 teaspoon of garlic (minced)
- 1 teaspoon of ginger (minced)
- 1 teaspoon of ground black pepper

Steps

1. Combine and mix all the ingredients.
2. Let it stand for 1 hour before marinating the meat.

* In Hawaii, soy sauce is known as shoyu sauce. For best tasting shoyu chicken, use Yamasa soy sauce.

Fighting for the Frying Pan

"Just a short note to compliment your Hayward store for their excellent service, delicious food and great attitude! They did a great catering order for Mother's Day lunch on a short notice." Vickie, Fremont

Lemon Chicken Sauce

Serves 5 to 6 people

Ingredients

- 1/2 cup vinegar
- 1/2 cup of sugar
- 1 cup of water
- 1/2 teaspoon of salt
- 2 teaspoons of corn starch
- 1 small piece of ginger (smashed)
- Dash of yellow food coloring
- 1 teaspoon of lemon extract

Steps

1. Combine and mix ingredients except lemon extract in a small pot.
2. Cook over medium high heat.
3. Stir constantly until it is boiling.
4. Turn off heat.
5. Stir in lemon extract.

Mahalo Means THANK YOU, not TRASH

"I am a loyal fan of your franchise and I am a regular customer at the Aurora location. They always greet me with an Aloha and Mahalo."
Bob, Colorado Springs

Meat Jun Sauce

Serves 2 to 3 people

Ingredients

- 1/2 cup shoyu or low sodium soy sauce
- 4 tablespoons vinegar
- 3 tablespoons hoisin sauce
- 2 stalks green onion, finely chopped
- 2 cloves garlic, minced

Steps

1. Place all ingredients into bowl and mix well.

All Coupons Accepted

"This is our second military assignment to Hawaii and we were sooooo excited to see your restaurant right next to our hotel in Waikiki. If you move East, do not call BBQ. They are very proud and territorial about barbecue there." Matt, San Diego

Hawaiian Chili Pepper Water

Serves 4 to 6 people

Ingredients

- 6 to 10 red chili peppers
- 2 garlic cloves (chopped)
- 2 teaspoons of freshly grated ginger
- 2 teaspoons of white vinegar
- 1 teaspoon of Hawaiian salt
- 2 cups of water

Steps

1. Chop the chili pepper into small pieces.
2. Combine all the ingredients in a glass jar.
3. Add hot water and leave it overnight at room temperature.
4. Shake mixture in the bottle.
5. Keep refrigerated.

Da Boss' Secret Diet

"We used to live in San Francisco and ate at your Kearny Street location. Now we live in Albuquerque and we miss the plate lunch. Please open one here." Milli, San Francisco

Brown Gravy

Serves 5 to 6 people

Ingredients

- 1/2 cup of flour
- 1/2 cup of water
- 1 quart of chicken broth
- 1/3 cup of soy sauce
- 1/2 teaspoon of white pepper
- 1/2 teaspoon of garlic powder
- Salt

Steps

1. Combine and mix flour and water to make roux.
2. Put ingredients except roux in a pot and bring to a boil.
3. Slowly whisk roux into pot.
4. Add salt to taste.

Spamming…Hawaiian Style

"I LOVE YOUR EVERYTHING. GIVE ME FREE SPAM! Just kidding! I love you guys. I don't waste my money on your food."
Roland, Kalihi

Fried Rice

Serves 5 to 6 people

Ingredients

- 2 eggs (beaten)
- 1/4 pound of Chinese barbecue pork
- 4 to 5 cups of cooked rice (prefer day old rice)
- 1/8 cup of green onions (minced)
- 1-1/2 tablespoons of oyster sauce
- Dash of pepper
- Dash of Hawaiian or plain salt
- Vegetable oil

Steps

1. Fry beaten eggs.
2. Shred fried eggs into small pieces and set aside.
3. Heat pan with oil.
4. Put rice into pan and fry.
5. Combine the remaining ingredients and cook with high heat until ready to serve.

No Steal From Your Dog

"Thanks for giving me the food that I grew up on! It's my all time favorite. My favorite is the original at Liliha." Sam, Ewa Beach

Pancit Bihon

Serves 4 to 5 people

Ingredients

- 1/2 pound of lean pork roast or steak
- 1/2 pound of shrimp (peeled and deveined)
- Vegetable oil
- 4 cloves of garlic (minced)
- 2 cans of chicken broth
- 1/4 teaspoon of ground pepper
- 1/4 cabbage (shredded)
- 1 stick of carrot (shredded)
- 2 packages (8 ounces) of thin rice noodles (pancit bihon noodles)
- 2 green onions (chopped into 1/2 inch to 1 inch pieces)
- Lemon wedges

Steps

1. Slice pork thin.
2. Remove shell from shrimp.
3. Clean and cut shrimp into small pieces.
4. Sauté garlic in a pan.
5. Place pork in pan and cook until barely done.
6. Add shrimp to pan and sauté for 1 minute.
7. Add broth and pepper and bring to a boil.
8. Soak rice noodles in cold water for 10 minutes.
9. Drain the water and set aside.
10. Add rice noodles and constantly stir until noodles are heated.
11. Drain, sprinkle with green onion and serve with lemon wedges.

Beating the Doctor's Advice

"I love L & L Hawaiian food! And now there's healthy choices! Yes! I'm on a diet so that works out perfectly. Try the garlic shrimp." Zita, San Mateo

Macaroni Salad

Serves 5 to 6 people

Ingredients

- 1/2 gallon of water
- 1 pound of macaroni
- 1/2 cup of onion (diced)
- 1/2 cup of carrot (shredded)
- 3 cups of mayonnaise*
- 1/2 teaspoon of white pepper
- 2 teaspoons of salt
- 1 small can of oil based tuna (drained)

Steps

1. Put water into a pot and bring to a boil.
2. Put macaroni into the pot and boil for 12 minutes or until cooked.
3. Drain water and cool macaroni thoroughly.
4. Combine all remaining ingredients and chill for at least 1 hour.

* For best tasting macaroni salad, use Best Foods or Hellmann's mayonnaise.

Pidgin To Da Max

"I attend TCU and this is the first time that I've left Hawaii. How far would I go? I would ditch my final exams right now just so I could catch a plane to Oahu and eat some Chicken Katsu! I like eat local kine grindz alreadeh!" Virginia, Waialae Iki

Plain Saimin

One Serving

Ingredients

- 6 cups of water
- 3 to 4 ounces of saimin noodles*
- 2 teaspoons of saimin soup base
- 1 teaspoon of green onion (diced)

Steps

1. Put 4 cups of water into pot and bring it to boil.
2. Put loose noodles into boiling water for 1 minute.
3. Remove noodles and strain water.
4. Wash noodles in cold water.
5. Boil 2 cups of water.
6. Add and stir in soup base.
7. Add noodles to serve.

* For best tasting saimin, use Sun Noodle's products at 1933 Colburn Street, Honolulu, Hawaii 96819, telephone: 808-841-5808 or www.sunnoodle.com.

Chicken Katsu Comes First

"Just had your chicken katsu for lunch in Thousand Oaks. It was so ono! I was lucky to find local food on my vacation in California."
Alec, Honolulu

Tofu Musubi

One Serving

Ingredients

- 1 piece firm tofu (sliced like the size of Spam)
- 1 teaspoon of teriyaki sauce*[1]
- Vegetable oil
- 3/4 cup of steam brown rice
- 1 teaspoon of barbecue sauce*[2]
- 1/2 sheet of nori (seaweed)

Steps

1. Dip tofu into L & L teriyaki sauce.
2. Heat pan with oil and slightly fry tofu.
3. Put brown rice into a musubi mold.
4. Put barbecue sauce on top of brown rice.
5. Place tofu on top of molded rice.
6. Wrap nori around rice and serve.

*[1] See page 105 for the teriyaki sauce recipe.
*[2] See page 103 for the barbecue sauce recipe.

We Prefer Rack of Lamb

“I simply LOVE your restaurant and food! Carpinteria is a surf down between Santa Barbara and Ventura. If we had an L & L here in town it would be HEAVEN.” Scott, Santa Barbara

SPAM® Saimin

One Serving

Ingredients

- 6 cups of water
- 3 to 4 ounces of saimin noodles*
- 2 teaspoons of saimin soup base
- 2 slices of Spam
- 1 teaspoon of green onion (diced)

Steps

1. Put 4 cups of water into pot and bring it to a boil.
2. Put loose noodles into boiling water for 1 minute.
3. Remove noodles and strain water.
4. Wash noodles in cold water.
5. Boil 2 cups of water.
6. Add and stir in soup base.
7. Grill or pan fry SPAM® with oil.
8. Add noodles and SPAM® to serve. Garnish with green onion.

You can also make saimin with Hawaiian barbecue chicken, beef, short ribs, shrimp, etc.

* For best tasting saimin, use Sun Noodle's products at 1933 Colburn Street, Honolulu, Hawaii 96819, telephone: 808-841-5808 or www.sunnoodle.com.

What To Do With Leftover Turkey

"I miss my L & L plate lunch. This wahine needs some Loco Moco and Macaroni Salad with plenty gravy." Diane, Tracy

Haupia

Serves 5 to 10 people

Ingredients

- 2 cups of coconut milk
- 5 tablespoons of cornstarch
- 1/4 cup of sugar
- 1/8 teaspoon of vanilla
- 1/8 teaspoon of salt

Steps

1. Combine ingredients in a saucepan.
2. Cook over low heat.
3. Stir constantly until smooth and thickened (slightly increase heat).
4. Pour mixture into a 9" X 13" pan.
5. Let the mixture cool and refrigerate to set.
6. Cut haupia into 24 pieces.

L & L Chicken Katsu is Da Best

"The food is GREAT and always made to perfection for the tailgate. We are regular customers and will continue to be loyal." Elisia, Phoenix

Fried Haupia

Serves 5 to 10 people

Ingredients

- 1 egg
- 1 tablespoon of water
- Haupia
- 1 tablespoon of flour
- 3 tablespoon of cornstarch

Steps

1. Coat haupia with flour.
2. Remove excess flour.
3. Dip haupia* into egg wash.
4. Dust with corn starch.
5. Deep fry for 2 minutes or until light brown.
6. Place on paper towel to drain of excess oil.

* See page 127 for the haupia recipe.

Homesick Hawaiians

"I cannot believe that L & L serves shave ice in Alaska. It is crazy but it tastes ono." Ryan, Anchorage

Shave Ice

Mainlanders call them snow cones, but Hawaiians call them shave ice. The difference is that the ice in snow cones is made from crushed, rather than truly shaved ice, a subtle but important distinction. Japanese plantation workers who immigrated to Hawaii brought this traditional dessert with them. Now, shave ice is found everywhere in Hawaii.

No trip to Hawaii is complete until you taste shave ice and eat plate lunches at L & L Hawaiian Barbecue. Just ask President Obama and his family.

Ingredients

(If you do not have an authentic shave ice machine, try this quick home version)

- 3 to 4 cups of cube ice (crushed)
- 2 cups of water
- Syrup (various flavors such as strawberry, pineapple, coconut, etc.)

Steps

1. Place crushed ice and water in a blender.
2. Turn on blender until ice is completely crushed (do not blend ice into liquid).
3. If there is too much liquid, add more ice and blend again.
4. Put blended ice into a glass.
5. Pour your favorite syrup on top or make a popular rainbow flavor with a combination of different syrups.

Mrs. Obama's Balanced Hawaiian Diet

"Hey L & L!! I can't wait til you guys open up in Washington D.C. I am waiting." Ellice, Georgetown

Quick Serving Malasadas

Serves 2 to 3 people

Ingredients

- 1 can of Pillsbury Buttermilk Biscuit dough
- Vegetable oil
- Sugar

Steps

1. Thaw dough in room temperature.
2. Cut dough into 9 to 10 pieces.
3. Heat oil to medium high temperature.
4. Drop dough into frying oil.
5. Cook until dough is golden brown.
6. Place malasadas on paper towel to remove excess oil.
7. Roll malasadas in sugar and serve.

Overloaded Surfer

"Wearing da best L & L HIC board shorts ever made in Hawaii. Makes me feel hungry and heavy." Harry, Kalihi

Hawaiian Boiled Peanuts

Serves 3 to 5 people

Ingredients

- Salt
- 3 to 4 pieces star anise
- 2 to 3 pounds of raw peanuts

Steps

1. Fill pot with water.
2. Add salt and adjust the saltiness to your preference.
3. Add star anise.
4. Boil the water and simmer.
5. Add raw peanuts and stir every 10 to 15 minutes.
6. Cook for 45 minutes.
7. Serve warm or chilled.

Thank You Hawaii for Everything

"Eddie donated a million dollars to UH. I will keep eating at L & L even though I will gain weight. Keep up your good work." Norman, Waipahu

Banana Lumpia

Serves 5 to 8 people

Ingredients

- 2 to 3 large bananas
- 1/2 cup of brown sugar
- 1/3 cup of dark chocolate morsels
- 1/4 cup of water
- 2 tablespoons of flour
- 15 to 20 lumpia wrappers
- Vegetable oil

Steps

1. Cut bananas in half and then cut into 1/2 inch strips.
2. Lightly coat bananas with brown sugar.
3. Sprinkle 3 to 4 dark chocolate morsels over sugared coated bananas.
4. Make paste by combing water with flour.
5. Place banana on a wrapper.
6. Fold nearest wedge over fillings.
7. Roll wrappers with open edges.
8. Fold and seal edges with paste.
9. Heat vegetable oil in the pan and fry lumpia both sides are golden brown.
10. Drain with paper towel and serve.

About the Illustrator

Jon J. Murakami is a freelance cartoonist born and raised in Hawai'i. He is best known for his line of Local Kine greeting cards which depict humorous occasions & holidays in Hawai'i. His regular comic strips include "Calabash" with Honolulu Star-Advertiser, "Generation Gap" with Hawai'i Herald, and "Online Aloha" with Time Warner. Additionally, Jon illustrated several Hawaiian children picture and board books and self-published a comic book entitled "Gordon River".

Mahalo

Thanks to many vendors, distributors and food brokers who consistently offer the highest level of service, support and products to L & L Hawaiian Barbecue worldwide.

Vendors

Sun Noodle/S & S Saimin	Hidehito Uki
Keoki's Laulau	Gary Ishimoto and Mike Irish
Unilever	Teresa Wong and Jan Watanabe
Farmers Rice	Ed Kurtz
King's Hawaiian Bakery	Michael White
Loves Bakery	Wayne Yamaguchi
Senba	Hideo Funasaki and Kazumi Takenaka
Simplot	Monique Vetri
Upper Crust	Yaneth Cardineux, Tom Shea and Ken Lida
Yamasa	Ken Iida
Cargill	Bryan Shaver and Greg Jackson
Certi-Fresh	Mario Galaz
Costa Pasta	Kent "Buzz" Weisman
International Paper	Doug Detavis and Bill Messerly
Ventura Foods	Joan Nelson
Golden West	Tom Vilas
Pepsi	James Totland, Gary Yoshioka, and Ryan Fujii

Distributors

Hosoda Brothers	Satoru Hosoda
L & C Food Distributors	Lloyd Chen
Y. Hata	Russell Hata, John Smiley, and Lester Lao

Food Brokers

Innovative Foods	Craig Nagano
L. H. Gamble Co.	Ray Barry
Rainbow Sales	Elaine Miyagi

Index of Cartoon Stars

Are you one of the cartoon characters? I have listed some names that may or may not be in one of the cartoons. If you can identify yourself in any of the cartoons, I will be more than happy to send you a personalized and autographed copy of the cartoon. If your name is not listed but the cartoon character looks like you, please email (info@hawaiianbarbecue.com) me a copy of your photograph and I will be more than happy to do the same for you. - Eddie

A Neil Abercrombie, Tom Acebedo, Amy Agbayani, Angie Aguilar, Joseph Akana, Josie Akana, Larry Akana, Wilma Akana, Lito Alcantara, Dean Alegado, Edna Alikpala, Harry Alonso, Josephine Alonso, Alyna Andaya, Avalyne Andaya, Bryan Andaya, Mary Ann Andaya, Jennifer Aniston, Ernie Apple, Belinda Aquino, Scott Arakaki, Violeta Arnobit, Toy Arre, Rudy Arucan, Chio Ung Aut-Cai

B Alan Baia, Vince Baldemor, Ray Barry, The Beatles, Alec Beglarian, Andre Beglarian, Donna Beglarian, Elias Beniga, Joyce Bernardino, Justin Bieber, Chuck Boller, Juliana Bonilla, Dan Boylan, Colt Brennan, Betty Brow, Kobe Bryant

C Mel Cabang, Rudi Camello, Robin Campaniano, Peter Carlisle, Sonny Carpio, Stewart Carvalho, Evelyn Casamina, Flora Casamina, Roland Casamina, Santos Casamina, Ben Cayetano, Alan Chan, Bonnie Chan, Charlie Chan, Joe Chan, Shirley Chan, Gerry Chang, Juncay Chang, Lou Chang, Matt Chang, Jessica Chen, Jin Chen, Becky Cheng, Jim Cheng, Raymond Cheng, George Cheong, Margaret Cheong, Pam Cheong, Prescott Cheong, Jennifer Cheung, Tannia Cheung, Kenneth Chong, Rose Chong, Norman Chow, Tiffany Chu, Rose Churma, Ronnie Coleman, David Cordero, Mary Cordero, Adeline Corpuz, Erwin Corpuz, Tom Cruise

D Marvin Dang, Rodney Dangerfield, Marivic Dar, Guy Davis, Abraham Dela Cruz, Brandon Dela Cruz, Loreto Dela Cruz, Lourdes Dela Cruz, Howard Dicus, Maria Dicus, Maggie Domingo, Peter Dong

E Queen Elizabeth II, Scott Endow, Erika Engle, Maria Etrata, Renato Etrata, Christine Eugenio, Alfredo Evangelista

F Chow Yun Fat, John Henry Felix, Angeline Flores, Anthony Flores, Debra Flores, Eddie Flores, Eduardo Flores, Elaine Flores, Elisia Flores, Ellice Flores, Eric Flores, Frank Flores, Janet Flores, Jimmy Flores, Kim Flores, Lucky Flores, Margaret Flores, Marissa Flores, Mark Flores, Matt Flores, Mike Flores, Quentin Flores, Richardo Flores, Robert Flores, Betty Fong, C.K. Fong, Kanoe Fragas, Ryan Fujii

G Baby Gaga, Kelly Gan, Bill Gates, Melga Gendrano, Annie Glasier, Mike Glasier, Francis Goo, Justin Goo, Benjamin Gudoy, Vicky Gudoy, Caroline Guira, Shelly Guira, Lynne Gutierrez

H Guy Hagi, AJ Halagao, Patricia Halagao, Colleen Hanabusa, Russell Hata, Mark Hayashida, Danny He, Min He, Paul He, Shari Higa, Virginia Hinshaw, Ricky Hu, Shirley Hu, Pauline Huang, Tony Huwang

I Ken Iida, Mike Irish, Gary Ishimoto, Yuna Ito, David Iwamiya

J Michael Jackson, Chris Jangus, Kiki Jangus, Yanny Jiang, Dwayne "The Rock" Johnson, Angelina Jolie

K Danny Kaleikini, Christina Kam, Eva Kam, Hannah Kam, Johnson Kam, Lawrence Kam, Nadine Kam, Denise Kammerzell, Jon Kammerzell, Madison Kammerzell, Kim Kardashian, Rob Kardashian, Greg Kemp, Terry Kennedy, Yoshie Kennedy, Bill Kikuta, Paul Kikuta, Sandy Kikuta, Daniel Dae Kim, Ryan Kim, John Kotake, Karen Kotake, Ritchie Koyanagi, June Kuang, Mila Kunis, Ashton Kutcher, Georgia Kwan

L Cliff Laboy, Jimmy Lake, Daniel Lam, Denise Lam, Kevin Lam, Minh Lam, Anthony Langit, Sergio Lawas, Andrew Lee, Eric Lee, Henry Lee, Stanley Lee, Darolyn Lendio, Jay Leno, Kelsey Leon, Kyle Leon, Tito Leon, Vicki Leon, David Letterman, Annette Lewis, Jet Li, Samuel Li, Wei Dong Li, Richard Lim, Jeremy Lin, Lisa Ling, Ken Po Lock, Diana Lorico, Frankie Lorico, Howard Louie, Bryan Luke, Kathy Luke, Warren Luke, Jackie Lum, Jim Lum, Kam Lau Lum, Michelle Lum, Stephanie Lum, Tim Lum, Avery Lung, Kathy Lung, Julio Luy

M Mario Madelora, Jason Malicsi, Rock Mando, Bruno Mars, Floyd Mayweather, Earl Mente, Bill Messerly, Hui Mian, Rick Miano, Itula Mili, Bennette Misalucha, Elaine Miyagi, Richard Molina, Candace Molinaro, Dave Molinaro, Lani Moo, Joe Moore, Chuck Mori, Kaori Mori, Kiva Morita, Jon J. Murakami, Miyamoto Musashi

N Rick Nakama, Clarence Nishihara

O Barack Obama, Rick Olegario, Ashley Olsen, Mary Kate Olsen, Henry Ou

P Manny Pacquiao, Cathy Palpallatoc, Mariano Palpallatoc, Michael Pan, Grace Park, Rita Parwani, Edith Pascua, Roland Pascua, Russell Pascua, Michael Perry, Rick Peterson, Queenie Pham, Dr. Phil, Peggy Picano, Zegna Picano, Elvis Presley, Larry Price, Anita Pun, Baby Pun, Roque Pun, Sam Pun

Q Tess Quemado

R Spencer Reid, Jamil Rey, Zita Rey, Crystal Malicsi Rivera, Emily Roley, Vance Roley

S Colonel Sanders, Peter Savio, Rob Schneider, Kevin Serai, Rosa Serai, Stephanie Serai, Arsen Shahnazarian, Arsineh Shahnazarian, Hermineh Shahnazarian, Ruben Shahnazarian, BJ Shang, Evelyn Shang, Victor Sharov, Abbey Shaw, Stanfield Shek, Tommy Shi, Tony Shi, Keith Shimomura, Vinay Shiriwastaw, Dennis Shiu, Josephine Shiu, Lulu Shiu, Ken Situ, Steve Sofos, Richard Solomon, Steve Sombrero, Jack Soo Hoo, John Soo Hoo, Winnie Soo Hoo, Kaidee Soohoo, Keiko Soohoo, Kelli Soohoo, Nancy Soohoo, Norman Soohoo, Rachelle Soohoo, Chuck Sted, Bob Stetler, Eva Stetler, Wong Su

T Augie T, Lanai Tabura, Henry Tam, Irene Tam, Kaki Tam, Keke Tam, Sharon Tam, Wayne Tam, Phuc Vinh Tat, Khanh Thai, Kitty the Kitty, Jiaming To, Tommy Tong, James "JT" Totland, Dennis Tse, Mitchell Tse, Larry Tseu, Christine Tumilowicz, David Tumilowicz, Steven Tyler

V Gary Valenciano, Monique Vetri, Aldrin Villahermosa

W Gary Wang, Betty White, Mike White, Michelle Wie, Anyssa Wise, Courtney Wise, Jason Wise, Lori Wise, Gloria Wong, Kingston Wong, Preston Wong, Steven Wong, Teresa Wong, Willy Wong, Tiger Woods, Peter Wu, Wesley Wu

X Jun Xiao, Jeff Xue

Y Sai Yamagata, Wei Yang, Peter Yeung, Kimo Yi, Christine Yip, Gary Yoshioka

Z John Zhang, Joshua Zhao, Guang Hui Zheng

L & L Locations

Visit us at www.hawaiianbarbecue.com for the latest updates, specials and more!

ALASKA
Anchorage

ARIZONA
Phoenix

CALIFORNIA
Alameda
Anaheim
Antioch
Brea
Campbell
Carson
Cerritos
Chula Vista
City of Industry
Cypress
Daly City
Eagle Rock
El Segundo
Elk Grove
Fairfield
Fremont
Fresno
Fullerton
Gardena
Gilroy
Glendale
Goleta
Hawthorne
Hayward
Hercules
Huntington Beach
Irvine
La Habra
La Jolla
La Verne
Long Beach (E. Willow)
Long Beach (E. 7th St.)
Martinez
Millbrae
Milpitas
Mira Loma
Mira Mesa
Mountain View
National City
Newark
Northridge
Norwalk
Oceanside
Oxnard
Pacific Beach
Pacifica
Palo Alto
Pasadena
Pico Rivera
Pleasant Hill
Pleasanton
Point Loma
Rancho Cucamonga
Redondo Beach
Redwood City
Riverbank
Roseville (North)
Roseville (South)
Sacramento (Folsom Blvd.)
Sacramento (Northgate Blvd.)
Sacramento (Florin Rd.)
Sacramento (Mack Rd.)
Sacramento (Broadway)
San Bruno
San Diego (Eastlake)
San Diego (El Cajon)
San Diego (Palm Ave.)
San Diego (Carmel Mtn.)
San Diego (National Ave.)
San Diego (Euclid Ave.)
San Francisco
San Jose (Curtner Ave.)
San Jose (Berryessa Rd.)
San Jose (Coleman Ave.)
San Jose (Capitol Expy.)
San Jose (Almaden Expy.)
San Marcos
San Mateo
Santa Clara
Santa Clarita
Santa Cruz
Santa Monica
Santee
Simi Valley
Stockton
Thousand Oaks
Torrance
Tracy
Union City
Vacaville
Vallejo
Vallejo (Downtown)
Van Nuys
Victorville
Walnut
West Covina
Westminster

TEXAS
Plano

COLORADO
Aurora
Colorado Springs

NEVADA
Henderson
Las Vegas (Serene Ave.)
Las Vegas (Tropical Pkwy.)
Las Vegas (Maryland Pkwy.)
Las Vegas (Nellis Blvd.)
Las Vegas (Maryland & Sahara)
Las Vegas (Rainbow Blvd.)
Las Vegas (Charleston Blvd.)
Reno

NEW YORK
New York
Evans Mills

OREGON
Beaverton
Portland

UTAH
Provo
Salt Lake City

WASHINGTON
Federal Way
Lakewood
Lynnwood
Renton

HAWAII

OAHU ISLAND
Aiea
Aikahi Park
Airport
Dillingham
Downtown
Enchanted Lake
Ewa Beach
Ewa Town
Gentry Waipio
Haleiwa
Hawaii Kai
Iwilei
Kahala
Kailua
Kaimuki
Kaneohe Bay Shop. Center
Kaneohe Windward City
Kapolei
Keeaumoku
Laie
Liliha
Mapunapuna
Mililani Fast Stop
Mililani Town Center
Mililani Mauka
Moiliili
Old Stadium
Pearl City
Royal Kunia
Sand Island
University–Lower Campus
University–McCarthy Mall
Wahiawa
Waianae
Waimanalo
Waipahu
Ward Center

KAUAI ISLAND
Kapaa
Lihue
Waimea
Hanalei

MAUI ISLAND
Lahaina–Honokawai
Lahaina Cannery Mall FC
Lahaina Shopping Center
Kihei
Wailuku
Kahului
Kahului–Queen Kaahumanu Cntr. FC

BIG ISLAND (Hawaii)
Captain Cook
Kona
Kailua-Kona
Waimea
Ocean View
Waiakea
Keaau
Hilo
Pahoa

AMERICAN SAMOA
Pago Pago

CHINA
Humen

JAPAN
Tokyo

NEW ZEALAND
Auckland

About the Author

Is it possible for someone who flunked English and knows little about cooking to write a great cookbook? With Eddie Flores, nothing is impossible. He is an American success story. Eddie immigrated to Hawaii from Hong Kong when he was 16 years old. School was extremely challenging for him; not only did Eddie have to deal with a language barrier, he also had to live down the reputation of being stupid. Eddie had to repeat first grade twice as well as third grade and eighth grade. His first grade report card said that he spent the entire day dreaming.

But those days of dreaming made Eddie successful. Eddie has earned a Bachelor degree from the University of Hawaii and a Master degree from the University of Oklahoma. As owner of L & L Hawaiian Barbecue with over 200 locations worldwide, Eddie is a nationally sought after speaker.

This book reflects Eddie's unique, funny and entertaining way of "talking story" about his life and experiences in Hawaii and building his restaurant business, filled not only with humor, but also many of his personal favorite recipes.

Made in the USA
Lexington, KY
15 June 2017